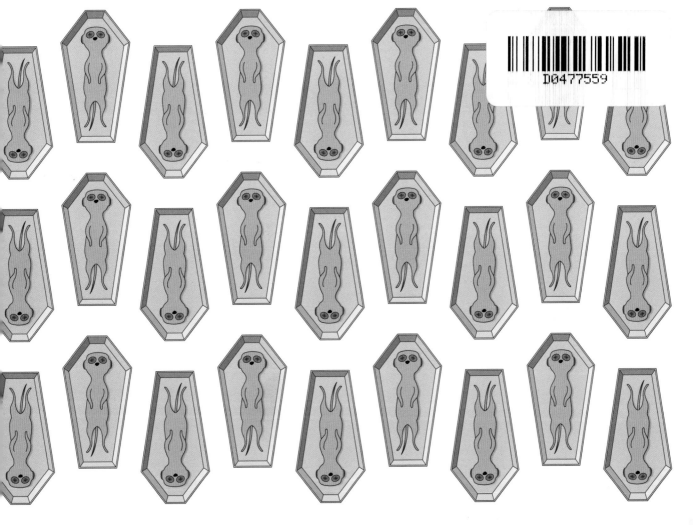

101 USES
FOR A DEAD
MEERKAT

From the same Author:

GUS & WALDO's BOOK OF LOVE, Orion 2006

GUS & WALDO's BOOK OF FAME, Orion 2007

GUS & WALDO's BOOK OF SEX, Orion 2008

GUS & WALDO CRAZY IN LOVE, Orion 2010

101 USES
FOR A DEAD
MEERKAT

Massimo Fenati

BOXTREE

First published 2011 by Boxtree
an imprint of Pan Macmillan, a division of Macmillan Publishers Limited
Pan Macmillan, 20 New Wharf Road, London N1 9RR
Basingstoke and Oxford
Associated companies throughout the world
www.panmacmillan.com

ISBN 978-0-7522-2792-4

3 5 7 9 8 6 4 2

A CIP catalogue record for this book is available from the British Library.

Printed by Printer Trento s.r.l.

Visit **www.panmacmillan.com** to read more about all our books and to buy them. You will also find
features, author interviews and news of any author events, and you can sign up for e-newsletters so
that you're always first to hear about our new releases.

Thanks to:

Jon Butler, Bruno Vincent, Simon Trewin, Walter Iuzzolino
and everybody at Macmillan

For Alda and Giorgio

Introduction

Prof. Anton P. Muskovitz, Professor of Meerkat Studies, Loughborough University

As a lifelong expert in the history and public understanding of meerkats, I have been asked many times over the last few years why it is that we have suddenly developed a fascination for this (admittedly rather 'cute') member of the mongoose family. When asked this naive question I always chuckle to myself, re-adjust my glasses to examine the person asking me the question, and pat them fondly on the bottom. Then I explain that the human fascination with meerkats is by no means a modern invention. Indeed, it stretches back to the very earliest recorded human history.

Paleolithic cave paintings, c. 27,000 BCE

Egyptian papyrus scroll, c. 3200 BCE

In some of the first cave paintings yet discovered, the distinctive upright frame of the meerkat can be spotted. Whether the animals were at that time a favourite food or a feared predator can be debated, but it seems undeniable that from the start humans were captivated by these strange upstanding creatures.

Even at the dawn of the written word, meerkats appear. In the 'Epic of Gilgamesh', the world's first work of literature, a wily meerkat is sent to kill the hero Gilgamesh as he sleeps in the desert, but the hero wakes just in time, kicks it to death, and makes soup from its entrails.

By the time of the great empires of Egypt and Rome, meerkats were often depicted in the great myths and stories of the time. There is record of Cleopatra making a present of some meerkat-skinned boots and gloves to Mark Antony before he set out on one of his campaigns, although after he heard rumours that they made him look effeminate, he had all meerkats in captivity within the Roman Empire drowned in olive oil. One starving Roman soldier, then stationed in Anatolia, skewered his meerkat with a stick and roasted it over the fire, carving flesh from it with a knife, and it is from here that the Turkish doner kebab is said to have gained its inspiration.

Illustration for a collection of poems by Opicinus Lucius Meerkattis, c.1107-1112

Sandro Botticelli, *The Birth of the Meerkat*, 1485

And thus it was, over the next two millennia of human civilisation. Meerkats were exported to Japan where they were respected as spirits and given special gowns to wear, while in the Renaissance, stuffed meerkats were often used as models when humans refused or were unavailable. By the time of Cubism, the naturalistic depiction of the meerkat's form was seen as outdated, and its depiction in art began to express the fracturing of the human's sense of the meerkat after the atrocities of the first world war and Freud's journey's into the subconscious (his publisher always refused to print his many great works on mongooses, and I have yet to attain access to his voluminous notes on the subject).

Anyway, I do go on, don't I. You would have thought from all this that I love meerkats. But I hate them! After forty years studying the little creatures, I can safely say that there is nothing more irritating than a meerkat. Standing there on his hind legs, twitching his little nose. Wriggling his little ears. He thinks he is so adorable! Ach! I spent an entire summer in the Kalahari desert in 1974, studying them and

Leonardo Da Vinci, *Meerka Tisa*, 1504

Pablo Picasso, *Meerkuenica*, 1937

hoping to be accepted into the clan. My costume was not totally convincing, I admit, and at twenty-three stone I suppose I deserved some of the funny looks I received at Johannesburg airport, especially as I was carrying two bottles of duty free and four hundred Bensons. I was determined to be a

Andy Warhol, *Campbell's Soup Can no.15*, 1962

method meerkat, you see, and to remain in costume at all times. After two weeks of agonising travel I arrived in the desert. I left six weeks later with sunburn, nibble holes in my ears, some strange tic that caused a terrible itching in my belowstairs, and a sense of humiliation that has never truly left. My findings — comprising notes and diaries — were lost, and the grant I had fought long and hard for from the Faculty of Bipedal Studies in the University of Loughborough was quite wasted.

The investigations of my illustrious colleague Massimo Fenati into the use of meerkats after death has been a solace to me, and with this book he has taken his researches to a new height. I hope you enjoy it, and I invite you to count how many of the suggestions in this book you had already made use of yourself. I counted eighty-six!

Prof. Anton P. Muskovitz
Weston-Super-Mare, 2011

101 USES
FOR A DEAD
MEERKAT

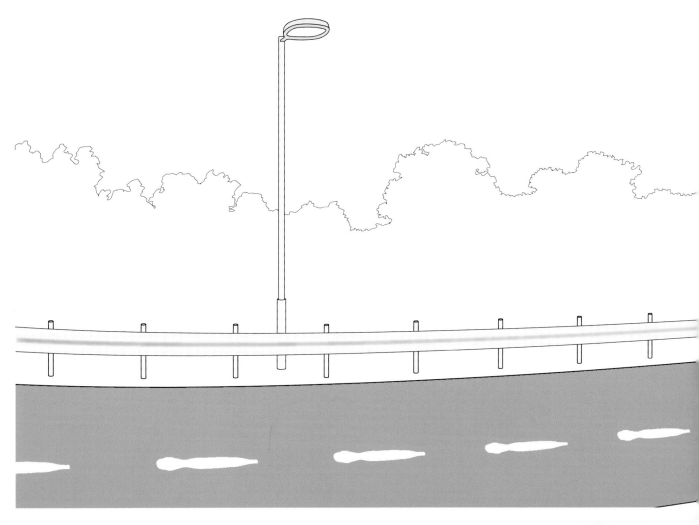

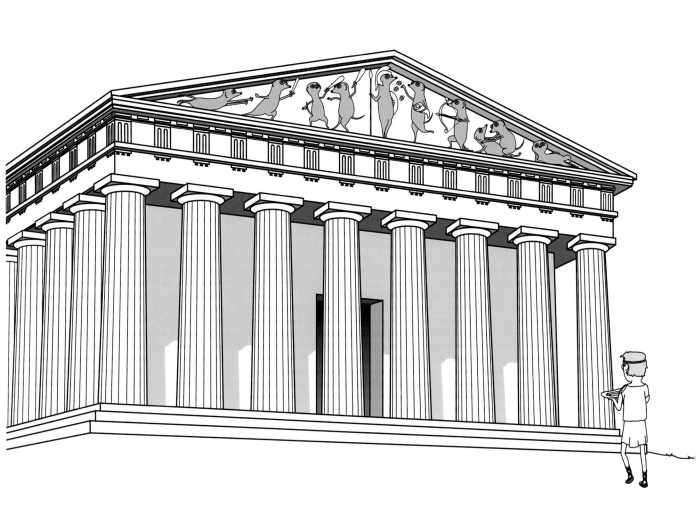

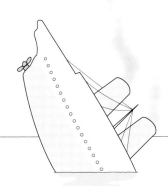

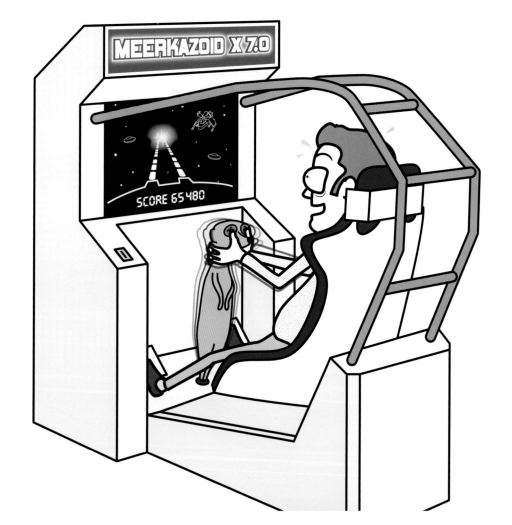

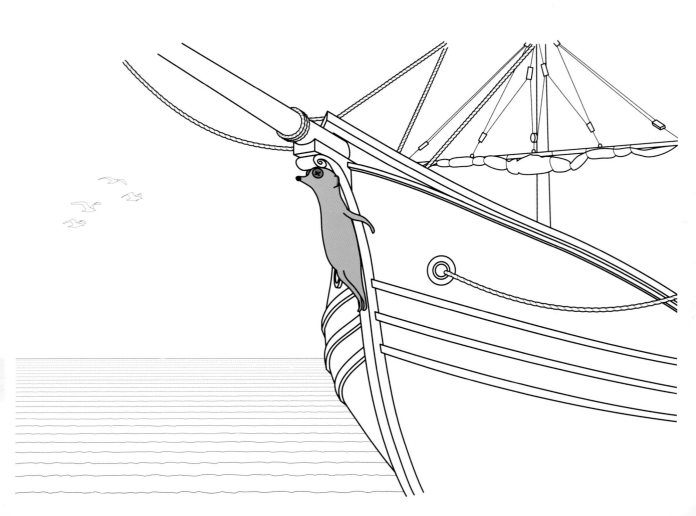

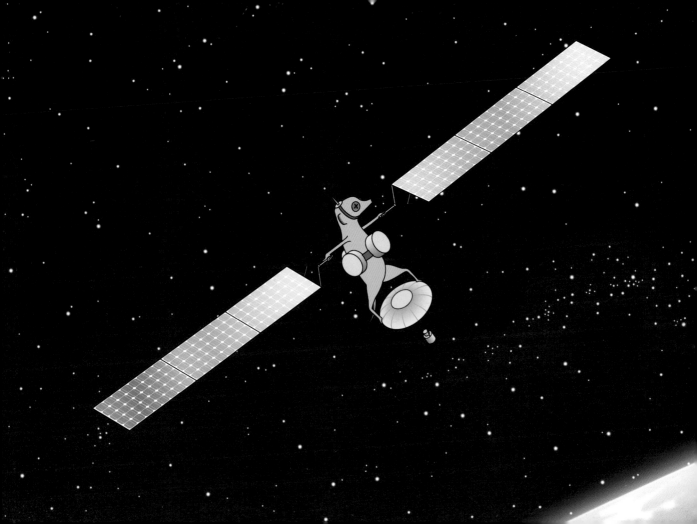

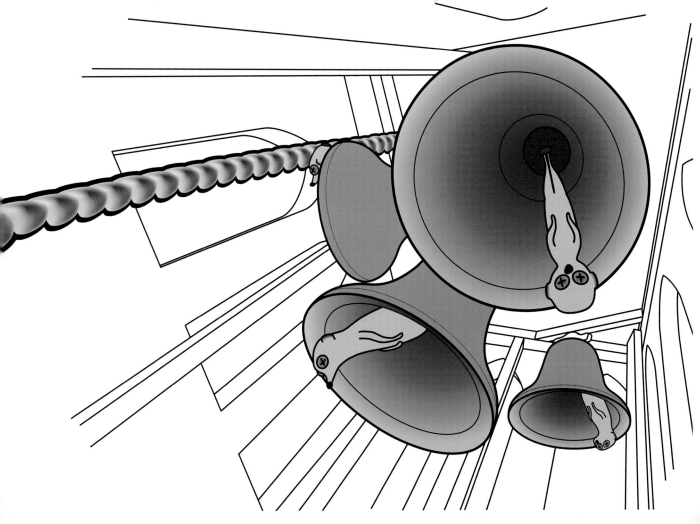

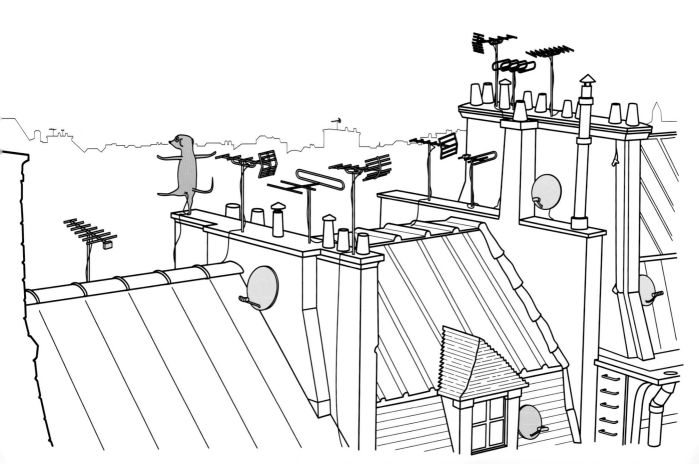

STARRING
DAVID HUSTLER-TOUGH

PAMELA BOOBIESON

NORM SCRAWNIE

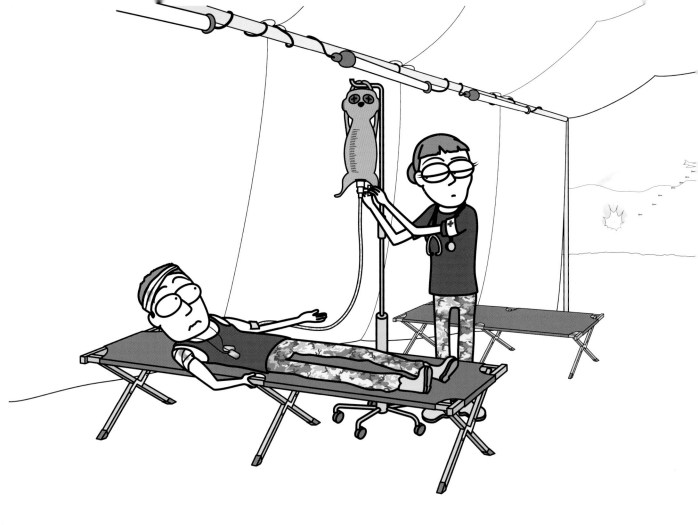

A Meerkat Bibliography

Suggested further reading:

The Meerkat: A Biography, Piotr Van Amsgaard (Verlaggesgruppe, Frankfurt, 1987)

Meerkats: An Illustrated History, Harry Spartacus (Phaidon, London, 1991)

Meerkat Madness: An Anthology, Anton P. Muskovitz (Macmillan, London, 1961)

More Meerkat Madness: An Anthology, Anton P. Muskovitz (Macmillan, London, 1963)

Yet More Meerkat Madness: An Anthology, Anton P. Muskovitz (Macmillan, London, 1965)

Meerkats Meerkats Meerkats, Anton P. Muskovitz (Michael Joseph, London 1967)

Why I Love Meerkats so Incredibly Flipping Much, Anton P. Muskovitz (Wheatfield Publications, Glasgow, 1969)

I Still Like Them, But Maybe Not Quite So Much as Before, Anton P. Muskovitz (Wheatfield Publications, Glasgow, 1977)

Now I Can't Stand Them At All, Really, Anton P. Muskovitz (Wheatfield Publications, Glasgow, 1985)

You Know What I Do, If You Mention Meerkats To Me? I Pinch Your Nose, Anton P. Muskovitz (Wheatfield Publications, Glasgow, 1992)

Fear and Loathing in the Kalahari, Hunter S. Thompson (Random House, New York, 1982)

The Discreet Charm of the Meerkats: An Erotic Odyssey, Alfred M. Puskovitz (Hamish Hamilton, London, 1999)

Meerkats in Beercans: my journey back from alcoholism, Anton P. Muskovitz (Yale University Press, Yale, 1975)

Near-Spats and Meerkats: the story of a marriage, Anton P. Muskovitz (University of Southampton Press, 1983)

Bedsit Doormats and Meerkats: Life after divorce, Anton P. Muskovitz (Local Biography Press, Godalming, 1985)

Sometimes It's Hard to Be A Meerkat, Anon (Heineman, London 1965)

Giving All Your Love to Just One Meerkat, Anon (Heineman, London 1965)

STAND BY YOUR MEERKAT!, Anon (Heineman, London 1965)

Oh Come on, Are You Seriously Still Reading at This Point?, Anon (Heineman, London 1965)

Yes, I Suppose You Are, Anon (Heineman, London 1965)

I Never Wanted to be a Bibliography Compiler, You Know, Anon (Heineman, London 1965)

My Mother Thought I Could Have Been a Concert Pianist, Anon (Heineman, London 1965)

She Was Probably Wrong Though, Anon (Heineman, London 1965)

Stupid Old Bag, Anon (Heineman, London 1965)

Author's Biography

Massimo Fenati was born in Genoa (Italy). After completing a master's degree in Architecture, he moved to London in 1995 and started to work as a product and packaging designer in some of Britain's most important design practices: Jasper Morrison, Pentagram, David Chipperfield Architects and more.

After several years of 3D design work, his career as an illustrator and animator started in 2006 when he published his first illustrated humour book in the UK: GUS & WALDO'S BOOK OF LOVE, which was followed by three more books in the same series (G&W'S BOOK OF FAME, 2007; G&W'S BOOK OF SEX, 2008; G&W CRAZY IN LOVE, 2010), later translated and published in several foreign countries.

With the animation based on these books, he won the Sub-Ti Short competition at the 2009 Venice Film Festival. His new short, 'The Gus & Waldo Show', won the audience awards at the 2010 IRIS Animation Festival in Rio de Janeiro and at the 2010 Queersicht Film Festival in Berne.

Massimo also produces graphic packages and title sequences for TV programmes for BBC, Channel 4 and Sky. He creates album covers and editorial illustrations for a number of publications. His most recent work includes the design of the image and logo for the 2011 edition of the Turin International GLBT Film Festival.

www.massimofenati.com

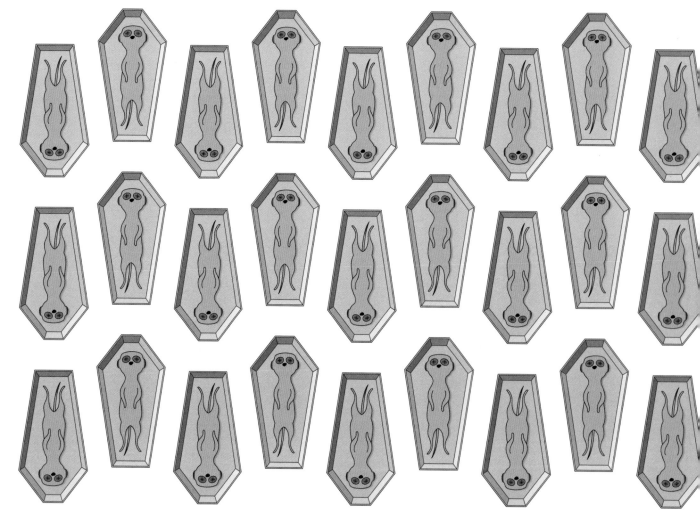